MEGALODON
THE PREHISTORIC SHARK

STEPHEN CUMBAA & SUSAN HUGHES
ILLUSTRATED BY RON BERG

ISBN: 1-58184-004-7
A B C D E F G H I J

Printed in Canada.

Art Direction: David Thorne
Communications

Somerville House, USA is distributed
by Penguin Putnam Books for Young
Readers, 345 Hudson Street, NY, 10014

Published in Canada by
Somerville House Publishing
a division of Somerville House
Books Limited
3080 Yonge Street, Suite 5000
Toronto, ON M4N 3N1

*To my brothers, Larry and Greg, with whom
I started collecting fossilized shark teeth on
the beaches of Florida, and whose love, good
humor, and camaraderie continue to be an
important part of my adult life.* — S.C.

*To my mother, whose depth of love and
support amazes and sustains me.* — S.H.

Authors' Acknowledgements
This book would not have been possible
without the published research and/or
help and advice of Michael Gottfried,
Robert Purdy, Shelton Applegate,
Leonard Compagno, John Maisey,
John Clay Bruner, Henri Cappetta,
Gerald Case, J.D. Stewart, Marc Frank,
Vincent Schneider, and Gordon Hubbell
and the efforts of collectors all over
the world who place their finds in museums.

Picture Credits
19 Nicholas Steno /
Nevraumont Publishing;
23 Bob Cranston / Mo Yung
Productions; 27 Marty Snyderman;
34 Chip Clark / Smithsonian Institution;
45 Hans Fricke / Max Planck Institute

Canadian
Museum of
Nature

Musée
canadien de la
NATURE

Special thanks for scientific consultation
to the Canadian Museum of Nature,
Ottawa ON, Canada

Contents

With jaws wide, Megalodon, the giant shark, begins a surprise attack.

4

Attack!

The dinosaurs have come and gone. Now three-toed horses and mammoth-like beasts walk the earth and the sea is alive with whales and fish. It will be millions of years before the first humans warm themselves by a fire.

A young whale, the length of a small school bus, feeds near the surface of the warm ocean. It takes water into its mouth, then strains the water through the fringes of baleen that hang from the roof of its mouth.

5

Left behind for the whale to swallow are the tiny plankton and small crustaceans that nourish it. All is well.

Or is it? The whale is not alone. There is a hunter on the move. It is one of the most fearsome predators ever to live, the giant prehistoric shark known as Megalodon. Bigger than the dinosaur *Tyrannosaurus rex* and more than twice as long as the longest great white shark ever measured, Megalodon is the ruler of the sea.

The solitary shark slices through the water in search of food. Suddenly, it turns. The predator's keen senses have alerted it to the distant whale. Immediately the shark speeds toward it.

Swinging its powerful tail from side to side, Megalodon torpedoes toward its target. The whale swims lazily on, unaware of the danger closing in on it. Within moments the hunter is within striking range, behind and below the whale.

In a flash, Megalodon raises its snout, dropping its massive lower jaw and pushing its upper jaw forward with powerful muscles. Rows of knife-like teeth are exposed. The shark's eyes roll back in their sockets for protection.

It pushes its lower jaw up and out, clamping its teeth onto the surprised whale. The shark swings its head and the front of its body violently from side to side. Its teeth, serrated on the edges like a steak knife, tear easily through flesh and bone.

Megalodon swallows, then bites again…and again…and again…

Finally the whale is gone.

6

Open Wide!

How does Megalodon compare with *Tyrannosaurus rex*, a prehistoric predator that lived before Megalodon? The fierce dinosaur may have been two stories tall, but its entire skull could have fit into the huge jaws of Meg!

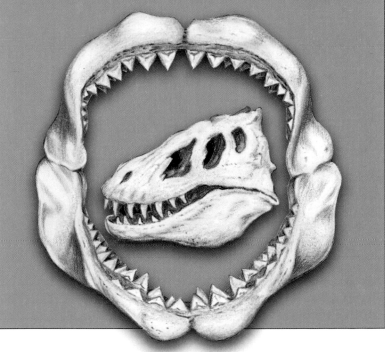

This ancient Megalodon tooth, about 5 million years old, was used to make your plaster Meg tooth.

The Mystery of Meg

No one alive today has ever seen the heart-stopping sight of Megalodon attacking and devouring its prey. That's because Megalodon, whose name means "great tooth," probably swam Earth's oceans from about 15 million years ago to 2 million years ago.

With only a few clues to go on, scientists still don't have all the answers to questions about this prehistoric giant. However, like detectives hot on the trail of a mystery, they are beginning to piece together the facts about Meg. In this book, you'll get the latest information and ideas that scientists have about this amazing shark.

Inside the sand block included in this kit, you'll uncover an exact copy of a Megalodon tooth. This plaster tooth is made from a mold of a real Megalodon fossil that is about 5 million years old. Read the instructions on the next pages and use the tool in the kit to unearth your own reminder of Meg, the great prehistoric shark!

A Deep Ocean Discovery

The year was 1873. The British ship *Challenger* was on a mission to find new plants and animals from the world's oceans. One day, during its four-year voyage, the ship dredged up two huge fossilized shark teeth from the ocean floor. Shark teeth had been found before, but not ones this big. Each tooth was about the size of a man's hand. *Challenger* had discovered something rarely seen before — Megalodon teeth.

It's easy to imagine the looks of amazement on the faces of the ship's crew as they held a Megalodon tooth in their hands. "How big was the shark that left this behind?" they must have wondered. Scientists have been trying to answer that question, and others, about Meg ever since.

How to Uncover Your Model Tooth

Before you start fossil hunting for the tooth included in this kit, find a table or floor to work on. (You can also work outdoors if the weather is warm and dry.) Be sure you have plenty of room, and cover your work area with lots of newspaper. It's best to begin this project on a day when you can spend at least an hour on it. Once you are ready, follow these steps:

1. Unwrap the block and put the plastic wrap in the recycle bin or garbage.

2. Pick up the tool and grasp the handle firmly, near the scraping edge.

3. Begin scraping along the edges of the block with the tool. You may have to experiment until you find a way of using the tool that works well for you. Tilting the block on its edge with one

hand and scraping down with the tool in the other hand, the way you peel a carrot, is one good way.

4. Continue scraping. It will take some time before you will see the tooth. Be patient — all fossil hunters have to be!

5. After you spot the tooth, scrape gently down, not across, the length of the tooth. Keep scraping until the whole tooth is uncovered. This will take quite a while.

6. When the tooth is loose, pull it out of the block. Use a soft cloth to wipe the tooth clean.

Now that you have uncovered your tooth, read on and discover what scientists have learned about Meg from the fossilized teeth they have found!

CAUTION!

If you are working near another person, be careful never to scrape toward him or her. Always watch out for flying chips. Technicians who clean and prepare fossils in museums always wear safety goggles. This is a good precaution to avoid injury to your eyes.

Colorful Teeth

The teeth of all living sharks are white, but fossilized shark teeth are not. A fossilized tooth gets its color from the minerals in the earth where it was buried. Most Meg teeth are gray, but others have been found that are black, chocolate colored, and blue-gray. Some teeth even appear light orange in places!

The Dirt on Fossils

To learn about living sharks, biologists usually find the sharks and study them. With extinct sharks, like Meg, the scientists' job is more difficult. That's where paleontologists come in. They are scientists specially trained to study forms of life that lived long ago.

One way that paleontologists learn about some extinct animals is by digging up and studying fossils of them. Fossils form after an animal dies. Most often, the soft parts of a dead animal rot away, and only its solid, hard bones are left behind. Over time, the bones get covered with

The paleontologist's tools: geological hammer, dental pick, brush, awl, and trowel.

earth. Water, carrying minerals from the earth with it, seeps into the bones. Slowly the minerals fill up little spaces in the bones, until the bones are more mineral than bone. The animal's bones have become fossils.

Unlike many other animals, however, Meg didn't have a skeleton made of bones. Like all sharks, Megalodon's skull, the vertebrae that made up its backbone, and its skeleton were made of cartilage, the tough, flexible material that makes your own nose and ears movable.

Cartilage doesn't fossilize easily the way bone does. It is sometimes possible for a shark's cartilage to become fossilized, however. Cartilage has a hard outer layer made of thousands of tiny prisms. The prisms are calcium phosphate, one of the bone-forming minerals. If the conditions are just right, and these prisms stay together after the shark dies, a fossil can form. Fossilized individual vertebrae of Megalodon have been found on the coasts of the eastern United States, Belgium, and Japan. The discovery of these fossils has helped scientists learn more about Meg's body.

Many Fossils, One Meg

Over 130 years ago, near Antwerp, Belgium, city workers uncovered many fossilized vertebrae from a shark's backbone.

Paleontologists believe that these fossils are from a single, small Megalodon that was about 30 feet (9 m) long!

Megalodon probably made and lost over 10,000 teeth in a lifetime.

Teeth

Anyone?

"Thank goodness for shark teeth!" Does this sound like a strange thing to say? It isn't — if you're someone who wants to learn more about Megalodon. After swimming in the oceans for 13 million years, Meg left behind very little except some fossilized vertebrae and lots of teeth. Meg's teeth had a hard layer of enamel that covered a core of softer, bone-like dentine which fossilized easily. By studying Meg's teeth, scientists have been able to come up with lots of information and ideas about this shark — everything from its size to what it ate.

Megalodon left behind many teeth because, like almost all sharks, it had a permanent tooth-making factory in its mouth.

The inside surface of a shark's upper and lower jaws is lined with gums that usually hold six to eight rows of teeth. Sharks use only about two to three rows of teeth at a time, however. The other rows hold spare teeth.

Unlike human teeth, a shark's teeth aren't rooted firmly in its jawbone. Instead, they are set loosely in the shark's gums. A shark's teeth can fall out easily on their own or when it eats. But losing teeth is never a problem for sharks. Gum tissue acts as an escalator, moving new teeth into place near the biting edge of the shark's mouth.

Scientists studying modern-day sharks have learned that some species of young sharks replace their teeth about once a week. Adult sharks replace their teeth about once every four to six weeks. Information gathered from fossils shows that Megalodon lost and replaced its teeth the same way that modern sharks do. However, scientists still aren't sure exactly how often Megalodon replaced its teeth. Perhaps early sharks, such as Meg, didn't get new teeth as frequently as modern sharks.

Although Meg didn't use them all at once, it probably had between 280 and 336 teeth at a time. Not every tooth from the time that Megalodon lived has become a fossil. Still, there are probably many, many more fossilized Meg teeth out there for scientists to find and study as they try to learn more about Meg!

▶ A 1667 woodcut of Steno's illustration of a modern shark head and a fossil tooth.

Tongue Stones

Over 300 years ago, a scientist named Nicholas Steno noticed something strange. The teeth from a dead shark he was studying reminded him of strange stones called "tongue stones." For centuries, stones in the shape of pointed tongues had been dug out of the soft rocks in cliffs on Malta, an island in the Mediterranean Sea. Steno compared the tongue stones with the shark teeth and decided that the stones were not all stones — some were shark teeth, too. Steno was right. Some of the tongue stones are fossilized Meg teeth!

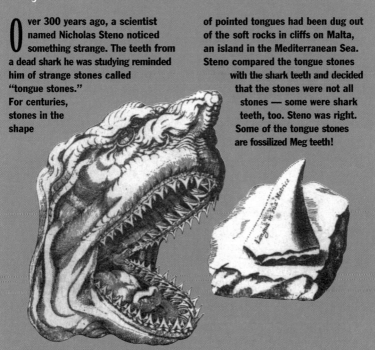

What could be
more scary than a
sea monster that
really existed!

When Did Meg Live?

It's fun to wonder if Meg swam the seas at the same time that early modern humans fished and swam there. Perhaps, around their fires, they told stories about a horrible ocean beast. Perhaps no one who saw the sea monster ever returned home to tell the tale. These things could have happened — or could they?

Like so much else about Meg, how long it swam Earth's oceans and whether it ever lived at the same time as early modern humans are mysteries that are still being investigated.

Some people believe that Megalodon survived into the last ice age. (There have been many ice ages on Earth. The most recent one began 2 million years ago and ended 10,000 years ago.)

The idea that Meg may have lived as recently as the last ice age has to do in part with the Meg teeth found by the ship *Challenger* (see "A Deep Ocean Discovery" on page 9).

In 1873, when *Challenger* dredged up two Meg teeth, each tooth was coated with a different thickness of a chemical called manganese dioxide. At first, scientists were very excited about this. They believed that manganese dioxide collected on objects on the ocean bottom at a known rate. They thought that finding out the thickness of this chemical deposit could help them learn how long the teeth had rested on the ocean floor. Scientists figured out that the tooth with the thickest coating had been at the bottom of the ocean for about 24,000 years. The tooth with the thinnest coating had been there for about 11,000 years. If scientists' calculations of the age of these teeth were correct, it would mean that Megalodon did exist at the same time as early modern humans. (Scientists already know that our own species, *Homo sapiens*, has existed for about 100,000 years.) However, now scientists question whether using manganese dioxide to figure out the age of objects is really reliable.

Meg teeth have also been brought up from the ocean bottom along with the bones and teeth of mammals known to have lived during the last ice age. Some people think that, because these fossils have been found together, the fossils must all be the same age. However, the

nets and dredges that pick up fossils of Megalodon and mammals from the last ice age also pick up fossils of animals that are known to have lived earlier than the last ice age. For this reason, scientists know that finding Megalodon teeth along with other fossils from the last ice age is not proof that Megalodon was still living then.

Most scientists think that the only certain way of dating Megalodon teeth is to find out the age of the rocks in which teeth are found. When scientists have done this, they've discovered that Meg fossils date back to 15 million years ago and up to 2 million years ago, before the last ice age began. The idea of Meg meeting early modern humans makes a great story, but today that's all most scientists think it is — a story, not a fact.

A Tale of Two Sharks

The largest Megalodons could have been 66 feet (20 m) long.

A re prehistoric Megalodon and the living great white shark related? When the first Megalodon teeth were found, scientists compared them with those of the great white shark and decided

the teeth of these two species were very similar. This led most scientists to believe, for many years, that the sharks must be closely related.

Many paleontologists thought that the great white shark was related so closely to Megalodon that it must have descended directly from

Meg. Early on, they placed the two sharks in the same genus (see "All in the Family" on page 29), *Carcharodon*, which means "jagged tooth." For nearly 100 years, the great white shark has been known as *Carcharodon carcharias* and the prehistoric giant has been called *Carcharodon megalodon*.

Then, about 30 years ago, paleontologists started to question the relationship between the two sharks. The scientists had always known that fossilized Megalodon teeth were much larger than any teeth of a living great white shark. The largest teeth of Megalodon are about as long as a man's hand. The largest modern-day great white shark teeth are only about as long as a man's thumb.

Meg teeth and great white shark teeth are different in other ways than just size. Scientists began to consider the other differences.

Just like a steak knife, the huge teeth of Megalodon are lined with hundreds of tiny, razor-sharp, saw-like serrations. These teeth were perfect for ripping Meg's prey to shreds. The teeth of a great white shark have cutting edges that are coarser.

All Megalodon teeth have a large, wide, V-shaped scar between the root and the enamel above the root. This scar is on the side of the tooth that faced the inside of the Meg's mouth. The teeth of the great white shark never have this scar.

The scientific arguments about the way Meg and today's great white shark may or may not be related focus on the teeth, the only real evidence. One group of paleontologists believes that Meg is only distantly related to the great white shark and is more closely related to other large, extinct sharks with finely serrated teeth. They would like to reclassify Meg as *Carcharocles megalodon*. Another group thinks that Meg and the great white shark are closer relatives, sharing a common ancestor. This group wants to keep the original classification, *Carcharodon megalodon*. The debate is still going on — in the journals scientists read, at meetings and conferences, and on the Internet!

▶ **A Meg fossil tooth dwarfs a great white shark tooth.**

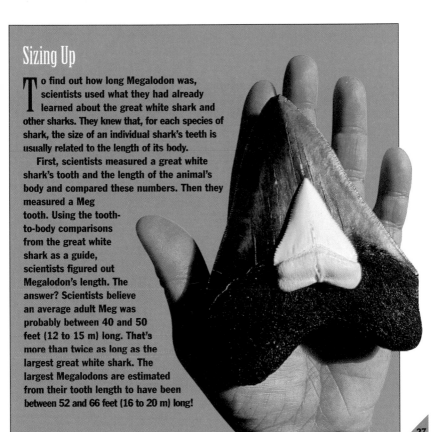

Sizing Up

To find out how long Megalodon was, scientists used what they had already learned about the great white shark and other sharks. They knew that, for each species of shark, the size of an individual shark's teeth is usually related to the length of its body.

First, scientists measured a great white shark's tooth and the length of the animal's body and compared these numbers. Then they measured a Meg tooth. Using the tooth-to-body comparisons from the great white shark as a guide, scientists figured out Megalodon's length. The answer? Scientists believe an average adult Meg was probably between 40 and 50 feet (12 to 15 m) long. That's more than twice as long as the largest great white shark. The largest Megalodons are estimated from their tooth length to have been between 52 and 66 feet (16 to 20 m) long!

27

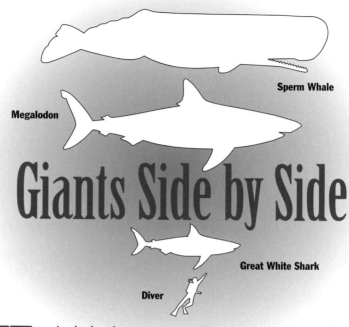

Sperm Whale

Megalodon

Giants Side by Side

Great White Shark

Diver

ere's a look at how Megalodon stacks up in size against the other giant predators of the sea. Although not as big as the record-breaking blue whale, the sperm whale is one of the world's largest living mammals and is *the* largest predator that has ever lived. The sperm whale can reach a maximum length of 65 feet (20 m) and a massive weight of 58 tons (53 t). It weighs as much as 13 large hippopotamuses and is probably five times as heavy as *Tyrannosaurus rex*.

Megalodon is the second largest predator and probably the largest shark that has ever lived. The largest Megalodons were most likely the females. (For most shark species, females are larger than males, although no one knows why.) The largest females were at least 50 feet (16 m) long, the length of three to four minivans placed end to end. A large female Meg probably weighed almost 53 tons (48 t), about as much as 12 large hippopotamuses. A large male might have weighed more than 37 tons (34 t), about as much as 8 or 9 hippos.

An average great white shark is about as long as one and a half minivans and can weigh as much as a small hippopotamus.

All in the Family

Scientists classify living things to understand the relationships between them. First, scientists decide which of the five main kingdoms a living thing belongs to. Living things are then divided and sub-divided into various groups that narrow down the classification. Here's how some scientists classify Megalodon.

KINGDOM:	Animalia
PHYLUM:	Chordata
SUBPHYLUM:	Vertebrata
CLASS:	Chondrichthyes
SUBCLASS:	Elasmobranchii
ORDER:	Lamniformes
SUBORDER:	Lamnoidei
FAMILY:	Lamnidae
GENUS:	*Carcharodon*
SPECIES:	*megalodon*

Super Survivor

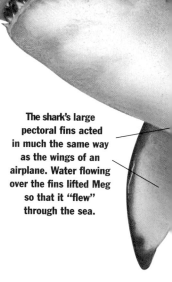

When Megalodon swam, all other animals probably hid, and for good reason. Megalodon's ancestors had been swimming the oceans for about 400 million years. As a group, sharks are so adaptable that they have become the ultimate survivors. Meg combined the best features of sharks with the biggest shark body ever. Here's what helped make Meg the ruler of the seas.

The shark's large pectoral fins acted in much the same way as the wings of an airplane. Water flowing over the fins lifted Meg so that it "flew" through the sea.

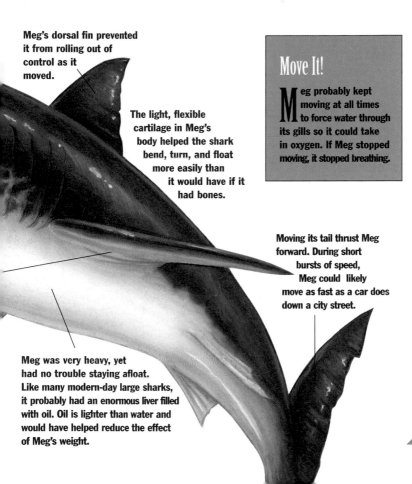

Meg's dorsal fin prevented it from rolling out of control as it moved.

The light, flexible cartilage in Meg's body helped the shark bend, turn, and float more easily than it would have if it had bones.

Move It!

Meg probably kept moving at all times to force water through its gills so it could take in oxygen. If Meg stopped moving, it stopped breathing.

Moving its tail thrust Meg forward. During short bursts of speed, Meg could likely move as fast as a car does down a city street.

Meg was very heavy, yet had no trouble staying afloat. Like many modern-day large sharks, it probably had an enormous liver filled with oil. Oil is lighter than water and would have helped reduce the effect of Meg's weight.

Uncommon Senses

Meg's nostrils enabled it to detect blood in the water.

Like all sharks, Megalodon the hunter probably had some of the best-developed senses of any animal that has ever lived. Meg's most important sense was its sense of smell. As Meg swam, water flowed through its nostrils to its nasal sacs. Odors in the water, such as the smell of fresh blood, caused signals to be sent directly to Meg's brain. At the first sign of blood, Meg sped off to find the source of the smell.

well as hearing with its ears, Meg probably "heard" its prey by means of a long, thin tube or "lateral line system" just under the skin along the sides of its body. Unusual vibrations in the water, such as those made by

Meg's lateral line system helped it "hear" its prey.

"ampullae of Lorenzini." With these ampullae, sharks can sense the direction and distance of prey they cannot see, hear, or smell.

Meg's ability to detect electric fields helped it to find prey and navigate.

an injured fish, would have caused the watery liquid and the tiny, hair-like receptors in this tube to move and alert the shark. Scientists think that sharks can sense vibrations over 1 mile (1.5 km) away. It's likely that Meg could do this, too.

Like all modern sharks, Meg probably had an extra ability — to sense the weak electric fields that all living animals produce. Sharks have hundreds of tiny pores on their snouts that lead to jelly-filled sacs called the

Getting Nosy

Sharks have a keen ability to smell blood. They can sniff out as little as five drops of blood in the amount of water needed to fill the average swimming pool!

33

Megalodon's massive jaws are about 6 1/2 feet (2 m) wide!

What's on the Menu?

With a mouth as large as a double doorway, Megalodon could think big when it came to meals. Scientists who have recently studied Meg's jaws believe that it could open them wide enough to fit in several big seals or a small whale!

It's likely that this prehistoric giant ate just this kind of prey. Megalodon probably hunted marine mammals — such as whales, manatees, seals, and sea lions — and large fish, including other sharks. Megalodon ate live or freshly killed prey. Perhaps it also ate dead animals that had been killed and partly eaten by other predators or had died naturally.

One way that scientists get information about Meg's diet is by looking at what a great white shark eats. When scientists have cut open dead great white sharks, they've found smaller sharks, young sea lions, seals, and sea turtles. One great white shark had two sand sharks in it, each about as long as an adult human! Great white sharks have also been known to eat garbage floating on the sea.

Paleontologists also look for clues wherever fossilized Megalodon teeth are found. Scientists have come across bones from seals, sea lions, dolphins, and whales that appear to have been bitten by sharks. In North Carolina, ancient whale bones were found with marks on them that match the size and cutting pattern of Meg teeth. It's likely that the whale, and others like it, fell prey to Megalodon's massive jaws and sharp teeth.

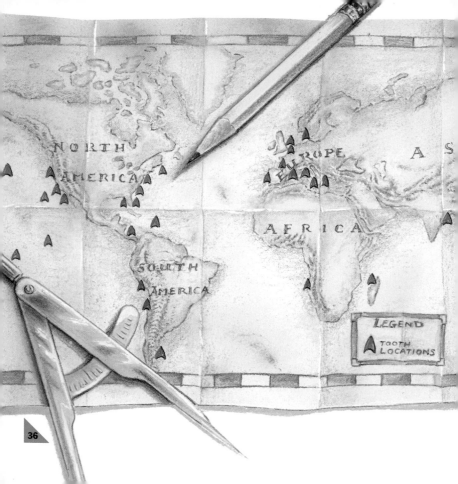

NORTH AMERICA

EUROPE

ASIA

AFRICA

SOUTH AMERICA

LEGEND

△ TOOTH LOCATIONS

Where Did Meg Live?

Some Meg teeth have been found inland where oceans once reached.

Here are the places around the world where fossilized Megalodon teeth have been found. Scientists think that these are likely the places where Meg also lived. All the areas are, or once were, oceans. This means that Megalodon was a saltwater, not a freshwater, shark.

Meg's Watery World

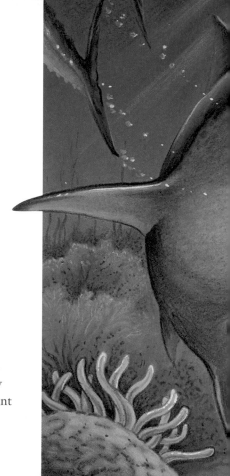

Scientists have used what they know about Megalodon and the oceans at the time Meg lived to help them learn more about Meg's surroundings. Here's what they think Meg's ancient environment (called a "paleoenvironment") may have looked like.

Sharing the Sea

Sharks and whales have shared the oceans for millions of years. They may seem to be very similar, but they're not. Here are some differences. All sharks are fish and take oxygen from the water through their gills. Whales are mammals and can breathe only air. Sharks have skeletons made of cartilage, while whales have skeletons made of bone. Sharks move their tails sideways while swimming. Whales move their tails up and down.

Long-nosed dolphin and tuna fled when Megalodon hunted.

A Pup Grows Up

An adult Megalodon was huge, so it's likely that Meg babies, called "pups," were big, too. A newborn pup was likely much bigger than, and

Female Megs outweighed the males by about 15 tons (14 t).

almost three times as heavy as, an adult human — between 6 1/2 and 10 feet (2 to 3 m) long and weighing up to 550 pounds (250 kg).

Most types of sharks have large litters, but scientists think that Megs were born in litters of two. Pups began life as eggs produced by a female Meg and fertilized by a male. The fertilized eggs hatched while they were still inside the mother, before the pups were born. A Megalodon pup probably grew inside its mother for almost one year.

A baby shark's life, even before birth, wasn't always easy. While inside the mother, developing pups would eat other pups. This type of cannibalism is sometimes seen in modern-day shark pups.

After birth, a Meg pup still wasn't safe. Although it could swim and look after itself right away, it was in danger of being eaten by an adult Meg, just as the pups of modern-day sharks are sometimes eaten by adult sharks. As well, a Meg pup had to watch out for other large, animal-eating sharks.

Scientists think that Meg pups were born and raised in "nurseries," places where a group of female Megalodons and their litters of pups gathered together. Nurseries were in warm-water areas that had a rich supply of food for the sharks. The adults probably ate baleen whales and many kinds of fish. The pups likely caught smaller prey and ate chunks of food left by adult sharks.

About 2 million years ago, killer whales thrived and Meg vanished.

Going, Going... Gone

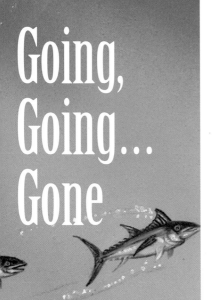

Why did Megalodon become extinct after surviving for millions of years? That's another question that has puzzled scientists. The best answer is that several different things together caused Meg's extinction.

Large baleen whales had become a big part of Meg's diet, but about 3 million years ago, the whales appear to have changed their habits. They began to migrate to the cold waters of the Arctic and Antarctic for part of each year. Migrating may have put the whales out of range of Meg, which swam and raised its young only in warm waters. With its main supply of food gone, Megalodon may not have been able to find enough other animals to eat and may not have been able to survive.

Killer whales were also evolving at the time Meg started to disappear. They may have been another one of the causes of Meg's extinction.

Scientists believe that prehistoric killer whales were relatively smart, as are modern-day killer whales, and likely were more intelligent than Meg. Ancient killer whales were about two-thirds the size of Meg, and it's possible that killer whales and Meg hunted the same prey. If killer whales were smarter, more successful hunters than Meg, and if they were increasing in number, then Meg might have run out of food and eventually become extinct.

Changing patterns of ocean currents may also have affected Meg. About 3 to 4 million years ago, the Isthmus of Panama, the land connecting the Americas, rose out of the sea. When this happened, the Pacific Ocean was blocked off from the Atlantic Ocean. Some scientists believe that a new current of cold, deep, North Atlantic water was formed during this time. The cold current traveled nearly everywhere around the world and affected the temperatures over the land nearby.

When the Atlantic Ocean began cooling, it caused temperatures, which were already slowly dropping over entire continents, to fall faster. Earth's climate began to cool and this may eventually have led to the last ice age. Perhaps Megalodon, a creature that lived in warm water, did not adapt to the cooler ocean temperature. The huge change to its environment may have led to Meg's extinction.

► **Until recently, scientists thought this ancient fish, called a coelacanth, was extinct.**

It's Alive!

I s there a chance that Megalodon may still live in the dark waters of the world's warmer oceans? Most scientists believe this is highly unlikely. For one thing, no one has ever found a tooth from a recent living Megalodon. All the Meg teeth that have been found so far are fossilized.

However, a creature is not necessarily extinct just because its fossil trail ends. An ancient fish called a coelacanth (SEE-luh-kanth) first lived on Earth almost 400 million years ago. Scientists believed that it died out more than 70 million years ago because no coelacanth fossils more than 70 million years old had been found. Then, surprise! In 1938, a live coelacanth was caught off the coast of South Africa. Since that time, other coelacanths have been found.

Join the Search!

There is still much to learn about the shark known as Meg, and the hunt is on for more evidence. You can join the search for fossilized Megalodon teeth and vertebrae by visiting some of the places listed below. Perhaps your finds will help scientists learn more about one of the most incredible sharks that ever lived!

In North America, the best places to hunt for fossils of Meg are along the east coast of the United States from Maryland to Florida and in some places on the coast of California.

The Calvert Marine Museum in Solomons, Maryland, has a reconstructed, life-sized Megalodon skeleton, as well as other exhibits about life in the ancient oceans. The museum also organizes fossil hunting on the public beaches of Chesapeake Bay and at nearby Calvert Cliffs.

Many of the best places to find fossils are areas where phosphate is mined. (Bones contain phosphate; where there are a lot of fossils, the earth is high in phosphate.) The Lee Creek open-pit phosphate mine near Aurora, North Carolina, has produced some of the biggest and best fossilized Meg teeth. Piles of Lee Creek earth have been placed outside the Aurora Fossil Museum, and visitors can search for shark teeth there. Also check out the North Carolina Museum of Natural Science in Raleigh, North Carolina.

The main public beaches in Myrtle Beach, South Carolina, and Venice, Florida, are other good places to find Meg teeth.

If you head out in search of fossilized teeth, be sure to follow these tips:

• Make sure you have permission before fossil hunting on private property or in parks. Fossil collecting is not allowed everywhere.

• Wear comfortable clothes, sturdy shoes, and a broad-brimmed hat to shade your eyes, and apply sunscreen to your skin.

• Use a sieve or piece of screen to sift through sand on beaches or in sandy areas. Digging usually isn't necessary. You can probably find more teeth just by walking and looking.

• Look for dark-colored, pointed, or triangular shapes. Fossilized shark teeth tend to have dark brown or black curved roots. Also keep an eye out for the more common teeth of smaller sharks and rays. These teeth may be as small as a fingernail.

• Bring a magnifying glass for a close-up look at your finds and small plastic bags to hold the fossils.

Remember that the best sources of information on good places to collect fossils are natural history museums and fossil clubs in the area that you want to visit. Also, libraries and the Internet are great places to search for information. Your Megalodon tooth is just a sample of the exciting fossil history of our planet!